W9-BHJ-979

DATE DUE

WHY SHOULD I TURN DOWN THE VOLUME?

✦ and other questions about healthy

eyes and ears ✦

Louise Spilsbury

Heinemann Library
Chicago, Illinois

Customer Service 888-454-2279
Visit our website at www.heinemannlibrary.com

Designed by David Poole and Tokay Interactive Ltd
Illustrations by Kamae Design Ltd
Originated by Ambassador Litho Ltd
Printed in China by Wing King Tong

07 06 05 04 03
10 9 8 7 6 5 4 3 2 1

Library of Congress Cataloging-in-Publication Data
Spilsbury, Louise.
  Why should I turn down the volume? and other questions about healthy
  ears and eyes / Louise Spilsbury.
      v. cm. -- (Body matters)
Includes bibliographical references and index.
Contents: Why should I take care of my eyes and ears? -- How do eyes and
ears work? -- Why shouldn't I put things in my ears? -- What should I do
about earwax? -- Why should I turn down the volume? -- What's an ear
infection? -- Do I need to clean my eyes? -- Why do my eyes get sore? --
Why should I wear sunglasses? -- Why do I have to take computer breaks?
-- Why should I use a reading light? -- Why should I have my eyes and
ears checked? -- Eye and ear facts.
  ISBN 1-4034-4683-0 (HC)
  1. Vision--Juvenile literature. 2. Hearing--Juvenile literature. 3.Eye--Care and hygiene
--Juvenile literature. 4. Ear--Care and hygiene--Juvenile literature. [1. Vision. 2. Hearing.
3. Eye--Care and hygiene. 4. Ear--Care and hygiene.] I. Title. II. Series.
  QP475.7.S65 2003
  612.8'5--dc21
                                   2003004976

Acknowledgments
The author and publishers are grateful to the following for permission to reproduce copyright material:
pp. 4, 14, 21 Getty Images/Imagebank; p. 5 Corbis/LWA: Sharie Kennedy; pp. 8, 20, 22, 27 Getty
Images/Taxi; pp. 9, 24 Tudor Photography; pp. 10, 17, 18, 19, 25 Science Photo Library; p. 11
Corbis/Bob Mitchell; p. 12 Corbis/Rob Lewine; p. 13 Corbis/Eye Ubiquitous: Robert & Linda Mostyn; p.
15 Corbis/Jose Luis Pelaez; p. 16 Trevor Clifford; p. 26 Corbis/Laura Dwight; p. 28 Corbis.

Cover photograph by Tudor Photography.

Every effort has been made to contact copyright holders of any material reproduced in this book. Any
omissions will be rectified in subsequent printings if notice is given to the publisher.

Some words are shown in bold, **like this.** You can find out what they mean by looking in the glossary.

CONTENTS

WHY SHOULD I TAKE CARE OF MY EYES AND EARS?

You have five **organs** of sense—eyes to see, ears to hear, a nose to smell, a tongue to taste, and skin to feel. Together, your five senses give you all the information you need to live and learn.

Your eyes and ears help you enjoy the world around you, but they also keep you safe. When you bike outside, your eyes enjoy the view and watch for road signs. Your ears hear your friends' voices and listen for cars.

Sight and hearing are probably the most important senses of all. Your eyes tell you what things look like and where they are, from the tiniest grains of sand to the biggest movie screen. Your ears listen for sounds as quiet as your cat purring or as loud as your friends shouting encouragement to you at a baseball game. Your ears also help you keep your balance.

Delicate organs

You should take care of your eyes and ears because they are delicate organs that can be easily damaged. They will work well only if you look after them properly. To keep them and the rest of your body healthy, you should eat a well-balanced diet with lots of fruit and vegetables and get plenty of sleep.

The old saying that eating carrots helps you see in the dark may not be exactly true, but fruits and vegetables do contain vitamin A, which keeps your eyes working well.

HEALTHY TIPS

Here are some tips for looking after your eyes and ears.

- Never put or poke anything into your eyes and ears, or anyone else's.

- Do not throw sand, stones, or dirt at other people, and do not let them throw these things at you.

- Never run while you are carrying scissors or other sharp objects.

HOW DO EYES AND EARS WORK?

Have you ever wondered how your eyes see and how your ears hear? The eyes and ears are complex and amazing parts of the body.

Eyes

When you look at something, the **cornea** at the front of the eye helps the eye focus on it. Light from the object enters the eye through the **pupil,** an opening in the middle of the **iris** (the colored part of the eye). The **lens** focuses the light onto the **retina,** a thin layer at the back of the eye.

The retina changes the light patterns it receives into signals. These signals travel to the brain along the **optic nerve.** The brain changes the signals into a picture.

When an image arrives at the retina, it is upside-down! The brain turns it the right way up.

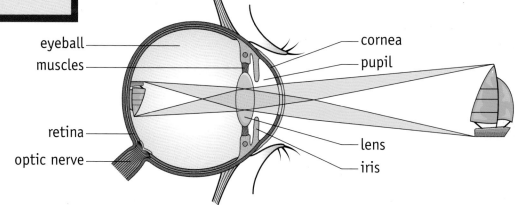

eyeball

muscles

retina

optic nerve

cornea

pupil

lens

iris

Ears

Sound makes the air **vibrate.** These vibrations are called sound waves. The **outer ear** catches sound waves. They pass through the **ear canal** to the **eardrum,** a thin skin stretched across the ear passage. When sound waves hit the eardrum, it vibrates. The eardrum is joined to tiny bones in the **middle ear** called **ossicles,** and they vibrate, too.

The ossicles pass the sound waves to a coiled tube in the **inner ear** called the **cochlea,** which is filled with fluid and tiny hairs. The sound waves move the hairs. The movements set off nerve signals in the **auditory nerve,** which goes to your brain. Your brain figures out what the signals mean so that you can hear what is going on.

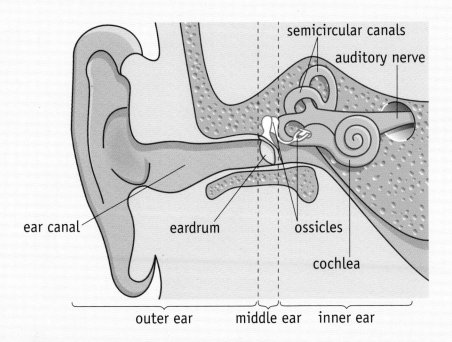

semicircular canals

auditory nerve

ear canal

eardrum

ossicles

cochlea

outer ear   middle ear   inner ear

Your ears have three main parts— the outer ear, the middle ear, and the inner ear. The **semicircular canals** are filled with fluid and hairs, and they help you keep your balance.

7

These children are able to balance like this because of the fluid in their semicircular canals.

WHY DO I GET DIZZY?

If you spin around on a merry-go-round for too long, the fluid in your semicircular canals keeps moving for a few moments after you stop. This makes you feel dizzy.

How do ears help me to balance?

Your ears help you balance by being aware of the smallest movement in your body. They do this using three bony tubes, called **semicircular canals,** found above the **cochlea.** They contain fluid that moves when you do. The fluid moves stalks linked to nerve **cells** in the canals, and this sends signals to your brain. The three different semicircular canals allow your body to sense different types of movement—side-to-side, up-and-down, and spinning.

WHY SHOULDN'T I PUT THINGS IN MY EARS?

An old saying goes, "Never put anything in your ear that is smaller than your elbow." Of course, no one is suggesting that you would even want to put an elbow in your ear, but the saying helps you remember that you should never put other things inside your ear.

Use a clean, soapy washcloth soaked in warm water to wipe around your **outer ear.** When you wash your hair, water will wash into your ears and clean them.

How can ears be hurt?

Some people stick cotton swabs or other things inside their ears to clean them out or to scratch them. However, it is very dangerous to poke around inside your ears with anything. The skin of the **ear canal** and the **eardrum** is very thin and fragile. These delicate and important parts can be injured easily if they are poked and prodded.

WHAT SHOULD I DO ABOUT EARWAX?

Earwax may not look very nice in your **outer ear,** but it has a very important job to do in protecting the delicate inner parts of your ear.

Earwax is the yellow, shiny, sticky stuff you sometimes see in your ear. It is perfectly normal and healthy to have small amounts of earwax in your ear. You do not need to do anything special to get rid of it. Washing your ears regularly is enough to keep them clean.

Where does earwax come from?

Special **glands** in the **ear canal** make earwax. (The scientific name for earwax is cerumen.) After wax is produced, it slowly moves through the ear canal toward the opening of the ear. Here, it dries up and falls out of the ear or is wiped out of your ear when you wash it.

What does earwax do?

Earwax protects against dirt and **germs.** It has special chemicals that kill germs that get inside the ear canal. This stops the germs from causing **infections.** Earwax also stops dirt, dust, and any other tiny particles in the air from getting to your **eardrum.** Particles stick to the earwax and get washed out with it later on.

WHAT IF EARWAX BLOCKS MY EARS?

If you think that you have too much earwax in your ears, you should see a doctor. Sometimes doctors give people ear drops, which help break down the earwax and get rid of it. Remember, though, that you should never put medicine in your ears unless a doctor tells you to.

Earwax also coats the inside of your ear with a waterproof layer. It makes water run out of the ear instead of letting it sit around to trap germs.

WHY SHOULD I TURN DOWN THE VOLUME?

If someone else can hear the music coming through your headphones, then it is too loud and may be damaging your ears.

We hear sounds all the time—from the TV, radio, traffic, and people shouting in the playground or chatting in the classroom. Most of the time, our ears can cope with all this noise. If sounds are too loud or go on for too long, however, your hearing can be damaged.

Loud sounds are bad

When you hear a sudden loud noise, such as fireworks, or listen to loud sounds for a long time, such as at a concert, some of the tiny hairs in the **cochlea** can be destroyed. Unlike other parts of your body, such as your skin, these fragile hairs cannot repair themselves. You have about 60,000 of these hairs, but each time you lose a few, your hearing works a little less well.

What happens to your hearing?

Some people lose their hearing for a short time after listening to loud noise. Others may get tinnitus. Tinnitus is when you hear ringing, whistling, or buzzing sounds in your ears. These things usually pass quite quickly, but your hearing weakens a little each time they happen. Do your best to avoid loud noises and protect your ears with earplugs when you cannot avoid them.

WHAT SOUNDS ARE TOO LOUD?

The loudness of a sound is measured in decibels. Sounds under 75 decibels should not hurt you, but listening to sounds over 90 decibels too closely for too long can damage your ears.

- Refrigerator humming: 40 decibels
- Normal conversation: 60 decibels
- City traffic: 80 decibels
- Front rows of rock concert: 110 decibels
- Military jet takeoff: 140 decibels

People who work with noisy machinery wear earplugs or earmuffs to protect their ears.

WHAT IS AN EAR INFECTION?

Many children get ear **infections**—in fact, most children have at least one ear infection before they are two years old! An ear infection is when **germs** get inside your ear and cause you pain or make you ill.

Outer ear infections

Outer ear infections are also called swimmer's ear because people who swim a lot often get them. You do not have to swim to get an outer ear infection, however. When water stays in the ear, it washes away the waterproof layer of earwax in the **ear canal.** The ear canal then stays wet instead of drying out. **Bacteria** can grow in damp areas like this. They cause an infection that makes your ear hurt. Doctors can cure the infection with medicine called antibiotics.

People who get swimmer's ear often have narrow ear canals that trap water easily. Wearing swim caps or earplugs can protect their ears.

Middle ear infections

Middle ear infections make your ear hurt and can cause fever and sickness. Children often get them when they have a cold. When germs get into the middle ear, your ear makes pus (a kind of fluid) to attack the germs. If you have a cold, the tube that usually takes fluids away from your ear—called the Eustachian tube—may be blocked with mucus. This makes your ear hurt. If you have pain in your ear, always have it checked out by a doctor.

Colds often cause ear infections. So try to avoid catching them! Always wash your hands before eating to get rid of germs that could get into your mouth.

WHAT IS GLUE EAR?

Glue ear happens when a sticky fluid (the "glue") blocks up the middle ear, making it hard to hear. To help, doctors can fit a tiny tube into the **eardrum** to take away the fluid.

DO I NEED TO CLEAN MY EYES?

Just like your ears, your eyes are delicate **organs** that should never be prodded or poked. You should wash the outside of your eyes, but your eyes have their own special system for keeping the insides clean—tears.

How should I clean my eyes?

You should wash around your eyes twice a day, in the morning and in the evening, when you wash your face. Use a clean washcloth and warm water and dry your face with a clean towel. Dirty washcloths and towels can spread **infections.** When you wake up, you may have a sticky or crusty substance in your eye. People call this "sleep." It is made up of tears with a little sweat and oil.

Your eyelids, eyebrows, and eyelashes catch sweat and other bits of dirt before they get into your eyes. Help them keep your eyes clean by avoiding dusty places.

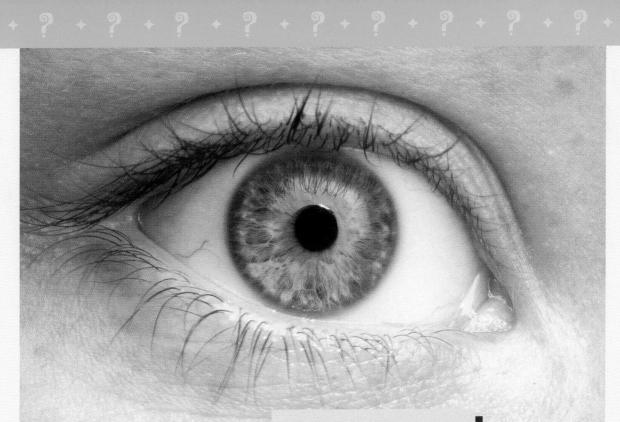

What are tears?

Tears are drops of salty liquid that come from **glands** in your upper eyelid. Every time you blink, a tiny amount of tear fluid comes out of the glands and washes over the eyeball. This tear fluid washes any dust or dirt out of the eye. It also contains a natural disinfectant that kills **germs,** and it stops your eye from drying out.

After tear fluid has washed over the eye, it leaves the eye through a tiny hole called the tear duct.

WHAT IF I GET SOMETHING IN MY EYES?

If you get something, such as sand or dust, in your eyes, do not rub them because this can hurt them. Your eyes will make extra tear fluid to wash themselves. If there is too much tear fluid to drain out of the tear duct, some of it flows down your cheeks, taking the dirt with it.

WHY DO MY EYES GET SORE?

Your eyes can feel sore for many reasons. If you have a cold, your eyes can ache and feel heavy. If you bump your eye or a ball hits it, you may get a black eye. This happens when the delicate skin around the eye is bruised. Sometimes people have sore eyes because of **infections,** such as sties or conjunctivitis.

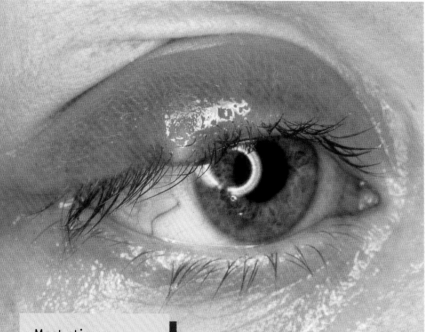

What are sties?

A sty happens when an oil **gland** in your eyelid gets blocked. This forms a red, painful lump on your eyelid that looks like a pimple. A sty usually fills with pus. If it becomes too big, it can make it hard to open your eye properly. Most sties disappear within a few days, when they burst and the pus drains away.

Most sties are harmless. You need to see a doctor only if you have a sty that does not go away by itself.

What is conjunctivitis?

Conjunctivitis is one of the most common eye problems for children. People also call it pink eye. It makes your eyes red, itchy, and swollen, and a sticky liquid collects in the corners of your eyes. Most children get conjunctivitis from **bacteria** that get into their eye. You can also get it when something irritating, such as dirt, gets in your eye. Your doctor will give you eye drops or ointment to put on the eye to make it better.

Conjunctivitis is easy to pass to other people, or from one eye to another, by touching. You can catch it by touching the hands of a friend who has it. The best way to avoid catching conjunctivitis and many other kinds of infections is to wash your hands often in warm, soapy water.

You should never use someone else's washcloth or towel when you have conjunctivitis because the infection can be passed on to other people.

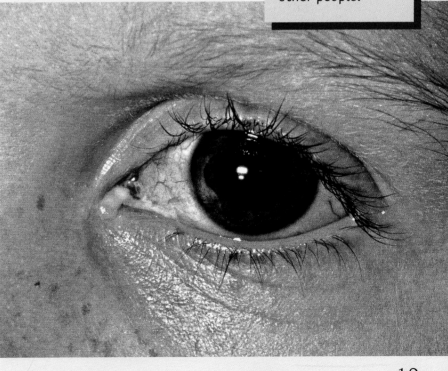

WHY SHOULD I WEAR SUNGLASSES?

The **retinas** at the back of your eyes can get burned. Your **pupils** get smaller in bright sunlight to prevent too much light from reaching them.

Have you ever wondered why your eyes try to close when you go outside on a bright day? They do so to protect themselves from the sunlight. Sunshine can hurt your eyes and the delicate skin around them. To be safe in the sunlight, you should always wear a pair of sunglasses.

How does the sun hurt my eyes?

Sunlight contains ultraviolet, or UV, rays. UV rays are like light, but we cannot see them. They are very strong, and they can cause eye problems, such as cataracts. Cataracts affect the **lens** of the eye. When you are young, your lens is clear. Cataracts are cloudy patches that can form on the lens as you get older. They make the world look cloudy and blurred.

What kind of sunglasses is best?

Look for sunglasses that offer 100 percent UV protection. These stop all of the dangerous UV rays in sunlight from hitting your eyes. Choose sunglasses with large frames that wrap around the sides to protect your eyes from all angles. If you play sports, choose glasses with shatterproof lenses, which will not break if you fall. Always buy sunglasses from well-known shops and ask for advice on which sunglasses fit you best.

WHY WEAR A HAT?

Sun hats help shade your eyes from the sun, and they protect your ears, face, and neck, too. Choose a hat with a brim all the way around, and make sure it is made from tightly woven fabric. Hats with holes in them let sunlight through.

Never look directly at the Sun, even if you are wearing sunglasses. Along with sunglasses, you should always wear a hat in the sun.

What other eye protection should I use?

Sunlight is not the only thing that can hurt your eyes. They can also be damaged if bits of wood, metal, chemicals, or other things get into them. To prevent this, you should wear protective safety goggles in woodwork and metalwork classes and when you do some science experiments.

It is also good to cover your eyes for some sports. Swimming goggles not only help you open your eyes underwater, they also protect your eyes from any **germs** floating in the pool. People sometimes wear shatterproof goggles to stop balls from hitting them in the eye in racket sports, such as tennis. Skiers often wear tinted goggles. These protect their eyes from UV rays and stop pieces of ice and snow from flying into their eyes as they ski.

Snow can reflect a lot of light. Tinted goggles stop the glare from hurting skiers' eyes.

WHY DO I HAVE TO TAKE COMPUTER BREAKS?

It is easy to lose track of time when you are using the computer, playing handheld video games, or watching television. You should take a break from these things every half an hour to rest your eyes so you do not strain (weaken) them. If you strain your eyes too much, you can damage your eyesight. Take a break, walk around, get a drink, or call a friend.

Look away from the computer screen once in a while and let your eyes focus on something else. This helps to keep your eyes healthy.

SCREEN SAVERS

Make sure that your computer screen is at least 20 inches (50 centimeters) away from your face. Also make sure that it is at the same level as your eyes. Prop it up with a couple of big books if you need to.

WHY SHOULD I USE A READING LIGHT?

When you read at night, always use a bright lamp that shines light over your book. Don't stay up too late, either. You need plenty of sleep to keep your eyes healthy.

When you read, write, or do anything in dim light, the **pupils** in your eyes dilate (get bigger). The eye muscles have to work to dilate the pupils so more light gets into your eyes and you can see properly. When you make your eyes work extra hard like this, you make them tired—and you may strain them.

Bedtime lights

When it is time to sleep, turn the lights off. Complete darkness helps your eyes get a good night's rest. It gives them a chance to recover from a hard day's work. If you cannot sleep without a light on, try to use a gentle nightlight rather than a bright lamp.

WHY SHOULD I HAVE MY EYES AND EARS CHECKED?

It is important for a specialist to check your eyes and ears. The earlier a problem is detected, the sooner it can be treated. You should visit an optometrist (eye doctor) for an eye test every two years. Most people go to the doctor about their ears only when they are worried about their hearing.

How does a doctor check my ears?

If you are at all concerned about your hearing, you should visit the doctor. The doctor will ask about your hearing and about any illnesses you may have had that might have affected it. He will look into your ear with a special light called an otoscope. If you have an **infection,** the **eardrum** looks red and swollen.

Using an otoscope a doctor can see if you have a blockage in your ear, such as too much earwax, that could be causing problems.

Other hearing tests

If the doctor cannot see an obvious reason for your problem, you may need to see an audiologist. An audiologist is a person who carries out special hearing tests. The tests are easy and do not hurt. In one test, you wear earphones and have to press a buzzer each time you hear a noise. If the audiologist finds that you have difficulty hearing, he or she can fit you with a hearing aid to help you hear better.

There are many different kinds of hearing aids. The kind this boy is wearing is worn in the ear.

HOW DO HEARING AIDS WORK?

Hearing aids work by making sounds louder. They pick up sounds through a tiny microphone and amplify them (make them louder) through an amplifier.
The amount of amplification a person needs depends on the kind and level of deafness they have.

What happens during an eye test?

Doctors trained to examine eyes are called optometrists. They check your eyes inside and out. They look at the outside of your eyes to check that your eyes move together properly and look healthy. Then, using a special device called an opthalmoscope, they look through the **pupil** of your eye. This lets them check that the inside of the eye is also healthy.

The optometrist will also ask you to look at an eye chart that is covered in different-sized letters. The doctor will cover each of your eyes in turn and will ask you to read out some of the letters on the chart. From these tests, the optometrist can tell whether or not you need glasses.

When an optometrist checks your eyes with an opthalmoscope, they can tell things about your sight, and they can spot other health problems, such as diabetes.

How do glasses help me see?

People wear glasses if the **lenses** in their eyes do not work well. A person who is short-sighted can read a book easily but cannot see things in the distance. A person who is far-sighted can see things in the distance but cannot see well close up. The lenses in glasses correct the problems in your eyes' lenses so you can see properly.

The lenses in a pair of glasses help you see. Instead of glasses, some people wear contact lenses on the surface of their eyes.

COLOR BLINDNESS

Optometrists may use special pictures made up of colored dots to check if you have color blindness. People who are color-blind cannot tell the difference between some colors. Red and green often look gray to them. This is because some of the **cells** on the **retina** are missing or do not work properly.

AMAZING FACTS

- Your eyes are always the same size from the moment you are born, but your ears never stop growing.

- It is impossible to sneeze with your eyes open.

- A stereo headset playing at full blast (about 110 decibels) can damage your ears in only half an hour!

- You blink more than 10,000 times every day.

- Sounds that are 90 decibels or louder, such as a noisy restaurant, a screaming child, or a lawn mower, can cause hearing damage.

- If you could lay out all the eyelashes that drop out of your eyes in a lifetime, they would stretch almost 100 feet (30 meters).

CARING FOR GLASSES AND HEARING AIDS

It is important to care for glasses and hearing aids as well as eyes and ears. Follow any instructions the specialist gives you and keep these tips in mind.

- Clean your glasses daily in warm, soapy water or with a lens cloth. Always put them away when you are not wearing them.

- Switch your hearing aid off when you are not using it, and store it in its box. Always keep it dry, and clean it with a dry cloth or tissue about once a week.

GLOSSARY

auditory nerve   pathway that carries signals from the ear to the brain

bacteria   tiny living things that can cause disease

cell   smallest building block of living things

cochlea   part of inner ear that looks like a snail shell. It changes sound waves into signals that travel along the auditory (hearing) nerve to the brain.

cornea   clear outer covering of the eye

ear canal   passageway that leads from the outside to the eardrum

eardrum   circular piece of skin (like a drum skin) that separates the outer ear from the middle ear

germs   tiny living things that can cause disease

gland   part of the body that makes substances for use in the body or to be ejected from it

infection   when germs get inside the body and cause disease

inner ear   part of the ear that contains the cochlea and the semicircular canals

iris   colored part of the eye

lens   part of the eye that focuses light onto the retina at the back of the eye

middle ear part of the ear that includes the ossicles

organ part of the body that has a particular function, such as the brain, ear, or eye

optic nerve pathway that carries signals from the eye to the brain

ossicles small bones that carry sound waves through the middle ear

outer ear part of the ear that you can see plus the ear canal, the passageway that leads to the eardrum

pupil opening that lets light into the eye. It looks like a black spot in the middle of the iris.

retina thin layer at the back of the eye that is connected to the brain by the optic nerve

semicircular canal three fluid-filled tubes in the inner ear that help you keep your balance

vibrate to move back and forth

FURTHER READING

Farndon, John. *Sound and Hearing*. Tarrytown, N.Y.: Marshall Cavendish, 2000.

Goode, Katherine. *Ears*. Farmington Hills, Mich.: Blackbirch Press, 2000.

Silverstein, Alvin, and Virginia B. Silverstein. *Earaches*. Danbury, Conn.: Scholastic Library, 2002.

INDEX